THE SANTA FE SCHOOL OF COOKING SERIES

Salsas

Susan Curtis and Kathi Long

Photography by
Lois Ellen Frank

GIBBS·SMITH
P
PUBLISHER

SALT LAKE CITY

This series of cookbooks is dedicated to the friends and guests of the Santa Fe School of Cooking, whose loyal support and patronage helped the school achieve success beyond anyone's wildest dreams.

First Edition
04 03 02 01 00   5 4 3 2 1

Published by
Gibbs Smith, Publisher
P.O. Box 667
Layton, Utah 84041

Orders: (800) 748-5439
Web site: www.gibbs-smith.com

Edited by Linda Nimori
Designed and produced by FORTHGEAR, Inc.
Printed in Hong Kong

Library of Congress Cataloging-in-Publication Data

Curtis, Susan, 1946–
    Salsas / Susan Curtis and Kathi Long ; photography by Lois Ellen Frank.— 1st ed.
        p. cm. — (The Santa Fe School of Cooking series)
    Includes index.
    ISBN 0-87905-948-6
    1. Salsas (Cookery) I. Long, Kathi. II. Title III. Series.

TX819.S29 C87 2000
641.8'14—dc21

                                                                00-024824

◎ CONTENTS ◎

Introduction iv

Salsas

Grilled Nopal and Poblano Chile Salsa 1

Tropical Fruit Salsa 4

Huitlacoche—Roasted Corn Relish 6

Roasted Tomatillo Salsa 7

Roasted Corn and Anasazi Bean Salsa 8

Tomatillo-Papaya Salsa 10

"Hold onto Your Hat" Habanero Salsa 11

Kumquat-Habanero Relish 12

New Mexico Red Chile Salsa 14

Tomatillo-Avocado Salsa .16

Pickled Red Onions 18

Mango Salsa 19

Grilled Pineapple Salsa 20

Bing Cherry—Pistachio Salsa 22

Jicama-Watermelon Salsa 24

Chicos, Posole, and Grilled Onion Salsa 25

Roasted Habanero Pickled Onions 27

Lemon Cucumber Salsa 28

Roasted Pepper Rajas 30

Roasted Pepper Relish with Raisins and Piñon Nuts . . .31

Grapefruit-Orange Salsa .32

Roasted Tomato Salsa 34

Salsa Fresca 35

Salsa Rouge 36

Olive-Tomato Salsa 38

Ingredients 39

Cooking Terminology and Equipment 40

Chiles 40

Resources 41

Acknowledgments 42

Index 43

Santa Fe School of Cooking and Market 44

INTRODUCTION

Salsa, the Spanish word for "sauce," can refer to an extremely wide variety of items. Salsas can be fresh (raw) or cooked, thick or thin, chunky or smooth, crunchy, hot spicy, mild, sweet, savory, tart, etc. They can be used as a side dish, sauce, condiment/relish, as an ingredient in other dishes, or even with a dessert. They can be made from vegetables, fruits, or a combination thereof, and are usually served at room temperature, but are sometimes chilled.

Whichever kind you choose, the impact of its flavor depends on the freshness or quality of the ingredients. When good-quality main ingredients such as tomatoes, tomatillos, or mangos are combined with accent ingredients, the result can be a salsa that has the ability to transform the simplest of foods into something fantastic.

Many of the salsas have chiles in them. We have rated the recipes in the following way: 1 chile = mild *(suave)*, 2 chiles = medium *(picante)*, and 3 chiles = hot *(muy picante)*. However, we encourage you to add chile to your taste. The heat level of each kind of chile may vary depending upon such growing factors as weather and soil conditions. Jalapeños are generally considered to be quite hot; however, in some instances, they can be quite mild. Thus, you will need to adapt the recipe to your taste and the heat level of the chiles you are using. If you desire no heat, omit the chiles.

Testing the recipes for this book has been a catalyst for festive parties. Whereas wine-tasting parties tend to be on the stuffy side, salsa tastings seem to bring out the revelry in guests. From Santa Fe's charming adobes to rooftops in the nation's capitol, parties have been given so guests could sample, critique, and enjoy the recipes in this book. Try it yourself. Mix some margaritas, make some tacos, grill some meat, and supply lots of chips to go with your salsas—you're on your way to a spirited party.

GRILLED NOPAL AND POBLANO CHILE SALSA

David Jones, an instructor in the culinary arts program at Santa Fe Community College as well as a chef and instructor at the Santa Fe School of Cooking, experienced this relish in Mexico. He recommends it as a side dish or a garnish for tacos, carne adovada, or grilled meats. South of the border, nopales are plentiful as well as economical.

Yield: about 1-1/2 cups

2 prickly pear cactus paddles (nopales), about 7 to 8 ounces

2 tablespoons vegetable oil

1 red bell pepper

2 poblano chiles, about 5 to 6 ounces

1/4 cup diced red onion

1 teaspoon minced garlic

1/4 cup chopped fresh cilantro

3 to 4 tablespoons extra virgin olive oil

2 to 3 tablespoons sherry vinegar

1/2 teaspoon freshly ground cumin

Coarse salt to taste

(continued on next page)

GRILLED NOPAL AND POBLANO CHILE SALSA

(continued from previous page)

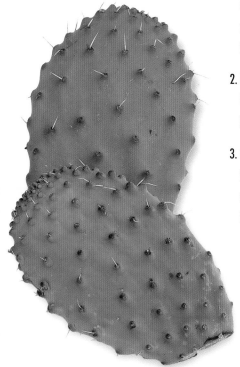

1. Lay a cactus paddle on a flat surface and run the blade of a sharp knife around the outside edge of the paddle from the narrow end toward the large rounded end and back down again, cutting off the cactus spines around the edges in the process. Then, slice the spines from the surface of the paddle one at a time with the tip of a sharp paring knife. Rinse the paddle and pat dry with paper towels. Repeat the process with the remaining paddle.

2. Brush the cleaned paddles with vegetable oil and sprinkle with salt. Grill over a direct flame until the skin is blackened in spots and the cactus paddle has softened slightly. Set aside to cool. Cut the cactus into quarter-inch dice. Set aside.

3. Grill the red pepper and poblano chiles and place them in a plastic bag to cool. Remove the skin, stem, and seeds from the pepper and chiles and cut them into quarter-inch dice. Mix the nopales, the pepper, and the chiles with the remaining ingredients in a bowl; let stand for 20 minutes before serving.

TROPICAL FRUIT SALSA

This summer salsa is a contribution from Peter Zimmer, one of our most creative chefs. Its flavors complement fish and seafood, but it would also pair well with grilled poultry, lamb, or barbecued game.

Yield: about 3 cups

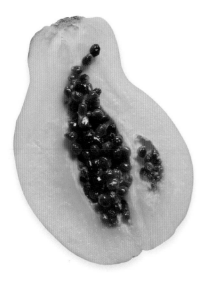

1/2 ripe papaya, peeled, seeded, and cut into quarter-inch dice

1/4 ripe pineapple, peeled, cored, and cut into quarter-inch dice

1 ripe mango, peeled, seeded, and cut into quarter-inch dice

3 fresh black figs, cut vertically into sixths (dried figs may be substituted if fresh are not available)

1 small red onion, peeled, cut into half-inch slices, charred over a flame, then chopped

1 red bell pepper, trimmed and cut into thin strips

Juice and minced zest of 1 lime

Juice and minced zest of 1 lemon

Juice and minced zest of 1 orange

1 tablespoon finely chopped fresh mint

1 tablespoon finely chopped fresh cilantro

2 to 3 teaspoons peeled and minced fresh ginger

1 tablespoon rice wine vinegar

1 tablespoon lime- or orange-flavored olive oil

Pinch of salt

Pinch of sugar to taste

1. Combine all ingredients and season to taste. Set aside for 20 minutes while flavors meld. Serve at room temperature or chilled.

Tip: This works well as a base for ceviche. Fold the diced uncooked fish into the salsa and marinate for 24 hours in the refrigerator. The citrus chemically "cooks" the seafood.

HUITLACOCHE-ROASTED CORN RELISH

The flavors of a simple roasted chicken or filet of beef would be greatly enhanced by this rustic, flavorful addition. Don't let the exotic ingredient (huitlacoche) keep you from trying this fabulous recipe.

Yield: about 2-1/2 cups

3 ears of corn
2 tablespoons canola oil
1/2 cup diced white onion
2 garlic cloves, roasted,
    very finely chopped
1 cup red wine
1/2 cup (4 oz.) canned or
    frozen huitlacoche

1 tablespoon juice from chipotle
    chiles in adobo sauce,
    or 1 tablespoon pureed chipotle
    chiles in adobo sauce
2 teaspoons fresh epazote,
    or 1 teaspoon dried epazote
1/4 cup cilantro chiffonade
Coarse salt and freshly ground
    black pepper to taste

1. Shuck the ears of corn and remove the silk. Roast the ears over direct flame, turning frequently, until blackened in places. Set aside. When the ears have cooled, cut the kernels from the cob and place them in a bowl. There should be about 1-1/2 cups.

2. Heat the canola oil in a skillet over medium heat. Add the onion and saute until golden, 4 to 5 minutes. Add the roasted garlic and red wine; reduce by half. Add the huitlacoche, chipotle chiles in adobo sauce, and epazote. Continue to cook over low heat, stirring frequently, for 8 to 10 minutes, until most of the liquid has evaporated. Remove from the heat and cool.

3. Add the roasted corn kernels and the cilantro to the "dry" mixture and stir to combine well. Season to taste with salt and pepper and serve at room temperature.

ROASTED TOMATILLO SALSA

This is one of many salsa recipes developed by Chef Kathi Long. In addition to being an instructor at the Santa Fe School of Cooking, she is a personal chef, restaurant consultant, and cookbook author. Kathi recommends this deeply flavored, rustic-looking tomatillo salsa as the ultimate sauce for cheese or chicken enchiladas. It is probably the favorite green salsa at the school.

Yield: 2-1/2 cups

1 pound tomatillos (about 10 to 12 medium), soaked, husked, and dried

2 to 3 fresh serrano chiles, stemmed

1 small white onion, peeled, cut into half-inch-thick slices, and separated into rings

2 to 3 garlic cloves, peeled

2 tablespoons olive oil

Coarse salt and freshly ground black pepper to taste

1/3 cup water

1/4 cup coarsely chopped fresh cilantro

Pinch of sugar to taste (optional)

1. Preheat the oven to 475 degrees. Position the rack on the second-highest level from the top of the oven. Place the tomatillos, serranos, onion rings, and garlic cloves in a bowl and toss with olive oil and a sprinkling of salt and coarsely ground black pepper. Pour the ingredients onto a foil-lined baking sheet, distribute evenly, and roast for 10 to 12 minutes, until the ingredients are soft and lightly browned. Remove from the oven and cool.

2. Coarsely chop the serranos, onion, and garlic by hand and place in a medium bowl. Pulse the tomatillos with their juice to a coarse puree in the food processor, then add to the bowl with the chile-onion-garlic mixture. Add the water and stir in the cilantro. Taste and adjust seasonings, adding a pinch of sugar if needed. Serve.

ROASTED CORN AND ANASAZI BEAN SALSA

James Campbell is the originator of this salsa that relies on the staples of southwestern cuisine—beans, corn, and chile. He grew up in a household of professional chefs, bakers, and exceptional home cooks. James has been teaching at the Santa Fe School of Cooking since 1998 and is the executive chef at El Farol, a popular Spanish tapas restaurant in Santa Fe. He recommends serving this corn-and-bean salsa with grilled meat or as a side to tamales.

Yield: 3 cups

2 ears of corn, husked
1-1/2 cups Anasazi beans, cooked, rinsed, and drained
2 jalapeño chiles, seeded and diced
2 tablespoons chopped fresh cilantro
3/4 cup diced red onions
2 garlic cloves, minced
1 tablespoon apple cider vinegar
2 tablespoons roasted peanut oil or toasted sesame oil
1 tablespoon brown sugar
Coarse salt and freshly ground black pepper to taste

1. Roast the ears of corn over direct flame and cool. Cut the kernels from the cobs. There should be about 1 cup.

2. Toss all ingredients together in a glass or stainless steel bowl. Taste and adjust seasonings. Let stand at room temperature for 20 minutes. Serve.

TOMATILLO-PAPAYA SALSA

Created by James Campbell, this light fruity salsa is perfect for grilled fish or seafood. Try seared scallops for a real treat.

Yield: 2-1/2 cups

4 tomatillos, peeled, rinsed, and cut into quarter-inch dice

1 ripe papaya, peeled, seeded, and cut into quarter-inch dice

2 serrano chiles, minced

1 small red bell pepper, cut into quarter-inch dice

1/2 cup diced red onion

1 tablespoon fresh lime juice

1 tablespoon fresh orange juice

2 tablespoons finely chopped fresh mint

1 tablespoon sugar, depending on the ripeness of the papaya

Coarse salt and freshly ground black pepper to taste

1. Mix all ingredients in a stainless steel or glass bowl. Taste and adjust seasonings. It is best used within a few hours and doesn't hold well for more than a day.

Tip: To use this as a more substantial side dish, add two to three cups of cooked basmati rice and season to taste with rice wine vinegar.

 # "HOLD ONTO YOUR HAT" HABANERO SALSA

Daniel Hoyer, restaurant consultant and seasoned chef at the Santa Fe School of Cooking, contributed this spirited salsa. He likes his salsas spicy, so beware! He recommends serving this with grilled shrimp, chicken, shredded beef, or pork tacos.

Yield: 1-1/2 cups

3 fresh habanero chiles
2 garlic cloves, unpeeled
1/2 medium onion, peeled and cut into half-inch slices
4 ripe plum tomatoes
Juice of 1 small orange
Juice of 1 lime
1 teaspoon dried Mexican oregano
1/4 cup chopped fresh cilantro
1 tablespoon olive oil
Coarse salt to taste

1. Roast the chiles, garlic, onion, and tomatoes over a direct flame until charred. Cool.

2. Peel the garlic and tomatoes. Remove stem and seeds and finely chop the chiles.

3. Place all the ingredients in the work bowl of a food processor and pulse, adding a few teaspoons of water as needed to yield a nicely spoonable consistency. Serve at room temperature or refrigerate until ready to use.

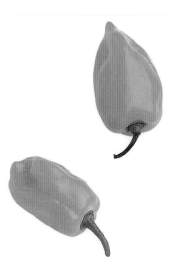

11

KUMQUAT-HABANERO RELISH

Zach Calkins pairs this unique relish with oysters on the half shell, lobster, or monkfish. It would also add an unexpected sparkle to holiday dishes such as ham or goose.

Yield: about 3 cups

12 ounces fresh kumquats, thinly sliced (about 3 cups)

1 habanero chile, stemmed and quartered

1 cup water

1 cup sugar

1/3 to 1/2 cup macadamia nuts, toasted and roughly chopped

2 tablespoons thinly sliced mint leaves

Pinch of salt

Squirt of fresh lime juice to balance the sweetness

1. Bring water and sugar to a boil. Add the sliced kumquats and the habanero and simmer until the liquid is reduced to a syrupy consistency, about 10 minutes. If the relish seems too thick, stir in a tablespoon or two of water to thin. Cool.

2. Fold in the nuts and the mint. Season with salt and lime juice to taste. Serve at room temperature.

NEW MEXICO RED CHILE SALSA

If you enjoy the smoky heat of chipotle chiles, this is the salsa for you. It's outstanding served on its own with tortilla chips, or with grilled pork or fajitas.

Yield: 2-1/2 cups

2 dried morita chiles or 2 tablespoons pureed,
    sieved chipotles in adobo sauce

8 dried New Mexico red chiles

4 medium-size ripe plum tomatoes

6 garlic cloves, unpeeled

1 medium white onion, peeled and cut into
    half-inch-thick slices

1 teaspoon crushed dried Mexican oregano

1/2 cup water

Salt to taste

Sugar to taste

Drizzle of extra virgin olive oil (optional)

1. Heat the broiler and set a heavy skillet over medium heat. Break the stems from the chiles and shake out the seeds. Place the chiles in the heated skillet, pressing them down with a kitchen towel until they have darkened in spots and you can smell their aroma. This process will take only moments. Place the toasted chiles in a bowl and pour very hot water over them. Weight them to submerge. Soak for 20 minutes, drain, and reserve the soaking water.

2. Spread the tomatoes on a foil-lined baking sheet and set on a rack positioned at the closest level to the broiler. Broil for 5 to 6 minutes, until softened and blackened. Using tongs, turn them over and roast for another 5 to 6 minutes, until softened and darkened on the other side. Cool, then peel the tomatoes, reserving any juices that accumulate and discarding the peelings.

3. Turn the oven down to 425 degrees. Separate the onion into rings. Spread the garlic and onion on a foil-lined baking sheet and roast until the garlic is soft and the onion is browned, about 15 minutes.

4. Chop the onion and garlic and set aside. Place the soaked chiles in a blender with a little of the soaking liquid; puree and reserve. Add the tomatoes and reserved juices to a food processor and pulse until coarsely pureed. Place the purees in a bowl and mix thoroughly. Add the oregano and water, if necessary, to give the salsa a pleasing consistency.

5. Taste and adjust seasonings with salt and sugar; drizzle with olive oil if desired.

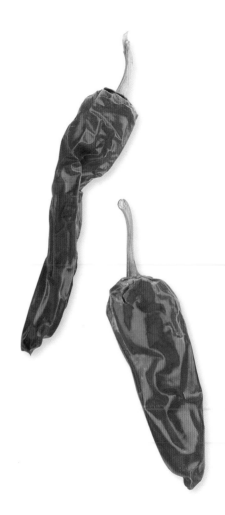

TOMATILLO-AVOCADO SALSA

The light fresh flavor of uncooked tomatillos adds an interesting twist to the familiar guacamole. Serve with tortilla chips, tacos, or fajitas.

Yield: 4 cups

1-1/2 pounds fresh tomatillos (about 12 to 14 medium),
soaked in warm water and husked
1 medium white onion, peeled and cut into quarter-inch dice
2 garlic cloves, peeled and minced
2 or 3 fresh serrano chiles to taste, minced
1/2 cup coarsely chopped fresh cilantro
1 large ripe avocado
Juice from 2 or 3 limes, plus more to taste
Salt to taste
Sugar to taste
Extra virgin olive oil to taste

1. Quarter the tomatillos and place in the work bowl of a food processor. Pulse to a coarse puree.

2. Place the tomatillos, onion, garlic, chiles, and cilantro in a bowl and stir to combine. Cut the avocado in half lengthwise, remove the pit, cube the flesh, and add to the tomatillos. Season with lime juice, salt, sugar, and drizzles of olive oil. Let stand 20 minutes. Taste and adjust seasonings.

PICKLED RED ONIONS

Use these to brighten up a salad of watercress, pink grapefruit, and avocado, or use as a garnish for any Mexican dish. They work great to liven up a sandwich too.

Yield: 2 cups

1 cup red wine vinegar

1/2 six-ounce can frozen orange juice concentrate, thawed

1/4 cup sugar

1 teaspoon dried Mexican oregano

1 bay leaf

Salt to taste

Extra virgin olive oil to taste

4 medium-size or 2 large red onions,
       peeled and cut into slivers

1. Combine all ingredients except the onions in a large bowl and stir until the sugar is dissolved.

2. Bring 4 cups of water to a boil and add the onions. Let them sit for 3 minutes, then drain. Add the onions to the vinegar mixture and set aside at room temperature from 4 to 24 hours. Stir the mixture and refrigerate, covered. The onions will keep for several weeks or more. Drain to use.

Note: this recipe is pictured on the back cover (upper photo, lower left).

MANGO SALSA

This is a wonderful garnish for grilled tuna or salmon, or any fish taco. It can also be used as a base for an excellent fish salad by mixing about one pound of grilled tuna or salmon into the salsa.

Yield: 3 cups

2 large ripe mangoes

1 medium hothouse cucumber,* cut into quarter-inch dice

2 medium red bell peppers, roasted, peeled, seeded, and cut into quarter-inch dice

1 medium red onion, peeled and cut into quarter-inch dice

1/3 cup coarsely chopped fresh cilantro

2 to 3 serrano chiles, minced

Fresh lime juice to taste

Salt to taste

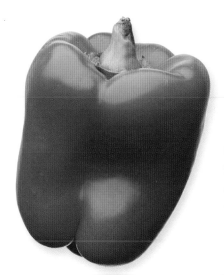

1. Peel the mangoes with a small sharp knife. Cut the flesh away from the large flat pit in two pieces, then cut it from the narrow edges of the pit. Cut these pieces into quarter-inch dice.

2. In a medium bowl, combine the diced mango, cucumber, red peppers, red onion, cilantro, chiles, lime juice, and salt. Toss gently but thoroughly.

3. Let the salsa stand at room temperature for 20 minutes to allow the flavors to meld. Serve at room temperature or slightly chilled.

Regular cucumbers may be substituted, but peel and remove the seeds.

Note: this recipe is pictured on page 21 (upper right).

GRILLED PINEAPPLE SALSA

This is a popular recipe with everyone at the Santa Fe School of Cooking because it goes well with so many things. Kathi Long suggests serving it with grilled salmon or tuna. It also works great with turkey and is a lively accompaniment for ham. If you can't find a ripe pineapple, purchase a slightly green one and leave it at room temperature for several days to ripen.

Yield: 2 to 2-1/2 cups

1 medium-size ripe pineapple, peeled, cored, and cut
    lengthwise into half-inch-wide strips

Olive oil

Coarse salt and freshly ground black pepper to taste

1 large red bell pepper, cut into quarter-inch dice

1 medium red onion, peeled and cut into
    quarter-inch dice

2 to 3 serrano chiles, minced

1/3 cup coarsely chopped fresh cilantro
    (reserve some sprigs for garnish)

1 to 2 tablespoons freshly squeezed lime juice to taste

Pinch of sugar to taste, depending on the ripeness
    of the pineapple

1. Place the pineapple strips in a medium bowl and season with olive oil, salt, and pepper. Grill the strips until nicely marked but not too charred. Set aside to cool. Cut the strips into half-inch dice and return to the bowl.

2. Add the bell pepper, onion, chiles, cilantro, and lime juice; mix well. Taste and adjust seasonings. Set aside for 30 minutes. Serve.

Tip: This is a basic recipe that works well with other tropical fruits. If ripe pineapple isn't available, substitute a ripe mango or papaya and avoid the mess of grilling.

Note: Grilled Pineapple Salsa (lower left) and Mango Salsa (upper right).

BING CHERRY-PISTACHIO SALSA

Zach Calkins, one of the more entertaining chefs at the Santa Fe School of Cooking, recommends serving this unusual fruit salsa with quail or game. It could also be incorporated into a stuffing for duck or goose, or used to garnish a cold soup of melon or cherries. It makes an excellent holiday accompaniment.

Yield: 1-1/2 to 2 cups

8 ounces fresh bing cherries, stems and pits removed,
    or 10 ounces frozen bing cherries, thawed
1/2 cup shelled, toasted, roughly chopped pistachios
1/4 cup cilantro chiffonade
1 tablespoon juice from chipotle chiles in adobo sauce
Pinch of coarse salt to taste
Pinch of sugar to taste,
    or 1 to 2 teaspoons of Spicy Honey Whip to taste
1 to 2 teaspoons fresh lime juice to taste

1. Roughly chop the cherries and stir in remaining ingredients. Season to taste with salt, sugar or honey, and lime juice. Serve.

JICAMA-WATERMELON SALSA

A lovely perfumed combination of ripe watermelon, crisp jicama, spicy chile, fragrant herbs, and vanilla, this recipe was developed by Peter Zimmer, a chef at the Santa Fe School of Cooking who opened the restaurant at the Inn of the Anasazi in 1990. It became an award-winning restaurant, which seems to be Peter's forte, as he has opened numerous award-winning restaurants around the country. Peter suggests serving this salsa with blackened salmon, barbecued pork tenderloin, chilled smoked jumbo prawns, or as a side salad.

Yield: about 2 cups

1 cup seeded and cubed ripe red or
   yellow watermelon
1/2 cup peeled and cubed jicama
1 small red onion, cut in thin slivers
1/4 cup New Mexico
   piñon nuts, toasted
1 ancho chile, stemmed, seeded,
   and cut with scissors into
   fine julienne
2 plum tomatoes, halved, insides
   scooped out, and shells cut
   lengthwise into thin strips

Zest of 1 orange
1 tablespoon mint chiffonade
2 tablespoons cilantro chiffonade
2 tablespoons rice wine vinegar
Seeds scraped from half a Mexican
   vanilla bean, pod reserved for
   another use
2 tablespoons Spicy Honey Whip or
   Red Chile Honey
1 tablespoon orange oil (optional)
Salt to taste
Sugar to taste

1. Combine all ingredients and let stand for 10 minutes.
   Taste and adjust seasonings. Serve well chilled.

CHICOS, POSOLE, AND GRILLED ONION SALSA

Peter Zimmer, the creator of this truly southwestern salsa, has earned the title of the "Picasso of Food" at the school, as he creates magic with food not only in flavor but in appearance. He suggests serving this salsa with grilled meats or pork mole.

Yield: 3-1/2 cups

1/4 cup red posole

1/4 cup white posole

1/4 cup blue posole

1/4 cup chicos

1 small red onion, peeled and cut into half-inch slices

1 small Vidalia onion, peeled and cut into half-inch slices

2 large garlic cloves, unpeeled

1 small orange

1 lemon

1 lime

1 red pepper, roasted, peeled, seeded, and diced

1 yellow pepper, roasted, peeled, seeded, and diced

2 tablespoons green pumpkin seeds, toasted

2 small canned chipotle chiles in adobo sauce, finely chopped, or 1 tablespoon pureed chipotle chiles in adobo sauce

Pinch of ground cumin

1/2 teaspoon ground coriander

2 tablespoons mint chiffonade

1/3 cup cilantro chiffonade

2 tablespoons olive oil

Salt to taste

(continued on next page)

CHICOS, POSOLE, AND GRILLED ONION SALSA

(continued from previous page)

1. Place the posole and chicos in a large saucepan and add 2 quarts of water. Bring to a boil and simmer for 2 to 3 hours, until the posole hulls have opened and the chicos are tender but chewy. Drain and rinse with cold water. Set aside.

2. Place the onions on a stove-top grill over a high flame and char lightly on both sides. Add the unpeeled garlic cloves to the flame and char on the outside. Set aside to cool. Peel the garlic cloves and mince. Coarsely chop the onions and mix with the garlic.

3. Juice and zest all the citrus fruits; fold into the peppers, seeds, chiles, cumin, coriander, the chiffonade of herbs, and olive oil. Then season to taste with salt.

4. Thoroughly combine the cooked posole, chicos, onions, and garlic with remaining ingredients in a medium-size bowl. Let stand for 30 minutes. Taste and adjust seasonings. Serve.

# ROASTED HABANERO PICKLED ONIONS

These onions are the perfect addition to all types of tacos and sandwiches. The addition of the fruity but **HOT** habanero chiles will give just the right amount of zing to the flavor.

Yield: 2-1/2 cups

1/3 cup good quality olive oil

2 large red onions, peeled and cut into thin slivers

2 fresh bay leaves

Leaves from 4 sprigs fresh marjoram

1/2 teaspoon dried Mexican oregano, lightly toasted

Coarsely ground black pepper to taste

Pinch of freshly ground allspice

1/4 cup balsamic or red wine vinegar

3 fresh habanero chiles, charred over a flame and chopped

Salt to taste

1. Heat olive oil in a large skillet over high heat. Saute the onions with the bay leaves for about 4 to 5 minutes, until lightly golden on the edges. Remove from the heat and stir in the marjoram, oregano, pepper, and allspice; combine thoroughly.

2. Stir in the vinegar and habaneros, and season to taste with salt. Set aside for 20 minutes. Serve at room temperature or chilled.

Note: this recipe is pictured on the back cover (upper photo, upper right).

27

LEMON CUCUMBER SALSA

Allen Smith, one of our newer chefs at the Santa Fe School of Cooking, discovered lemon cucumbers while visiting Santa Fe's Farmer's Market. At the time, he was living in New York City during what he describes as the "grilled meat and salsa rage." Allen created this recipe and thinks it serves as an easy way to "dress up" a simple piece of fish. It would also make a refreshing side salad.

Yield: about 2 cups

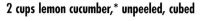

2 cups lemon cucumber,* unpeeled, cubed

Zest and juice of 1 lemon

2 green onions, trimmed and thinly sliced on the diagonal

2 teaspoons crushed red chile (chile caribe)

2 tablespoons chopped fresh herbs (a combination of

    chives, mint, tarragon, and/or cilantro is good)

Salt to taste

1. Combine all the ingredients and stir. Let stand for 20 minutes, taste, and adjust seasoning.

*Tip: Lemon cucumbers are named for their shape and color, which resemble lemons.
If you cannot find lemon cucumbers, peeled and seeded cucumbers may be substituted.

ROASTED PEPPER RAJAS

This salsa consists of roasted peppers and chiles cut into thin strips *(rajas)* and seasoned with sauteed garlic and fresh herbs. It is the perfect complement to grilled meats, fish, or pasta.

Yield: about 2 cups

1 red bell pepper, roasted, peeled, seeded, and cut into thin strips

1 yellow bell pepper, roasted, peeled, seeded, and cut into thin strips

1 orange bell pepper, roasted, peeled, seeded, and cut into thin strips

1 poblano chile, roasted, peeled, seeded, and cut into thin strips

2 large ripe plum tomatoes, halved, seeds scooped from the middle, and remaining shells cut lengthwise into thin strips

1 tablespoon chopped Italian parsley

1 tablespoon chopped fresh basil

2 tablespoons balsamic vinegar

Salt and freshly ground black pepper to taste

3 tablespoons extra virgin olive oil

2 cloves garlic, peeled and finely chopped

1. Place the pepper, chile, and tomato strips in a medium bowl along with the herbs, vinegar, salt, and pepper. Set aside.

2. Heat the olive oil in a small skillet over medium heat and saute the garlic until lightly golden and aromatic. Pour the oil and the garlic over the other ingredients and stir to combine well. Let stand for 10 minutes. Taste and adjust seasonings. Serve.

Tip: During recipe-testing for the book, there were often leftover salsas and other odd ingredients. By adding raw shrimp to a skillet with this salsa, heating it until the shrimp were cooked, and adding a final dollop of heavy cream, a scrumptious lunch was prepared with the leftovers. Most salsas, unless very vinegary, serve as a good base for sauteed shrimp, scallops, cubed chicken, or a bit of meat.

ROASTED PEPPER RELISH
WITH RAISINS AND PINON NUTS

This flavorful accompaniment enlivens pork tenderloin, lamb, or swordfish.

Yield: about 2-1/2 cups

1/3 cup golden raisins or currants

1/4 cup gold tequila

1 red bell pepper

1 yellow bell pepper

3 ripe plum tomatoes, cut into quarter-inch dice

1/3 cup thinly sliced scallions

2 tablespoons extra virgin olive oil

3 tablespoons diced red onion

1 cup diced zucchini or yellow squash

1 teaspoon minced garlic (optional)

1/3 cup New Mexico piñon nuts, lightly toasted

1/4 cup fresh herbs (basil, tarragon, cilantro, etc.), tightly packed and cut into chiffonade

2 to 3 tablespoons balsamic or red wine vinegar

Coarse salt and freshly ground black pepper to taste

1. Combine the raisins and tequila in a small saucepan and bring to a simmer over medium heat. Remove from the heat and set aside.

2. Char the bell peppers over a flame and place in a paper bag to cool for 10 minutes. Remove the skin, ribs, and seeds from the peppers and cut the flesh of the peeled peppers into thin strips. Cut the strips crosswise into quarter-inch dice and set aside in a small bowl. Add the tomatoes and scallions to the peppers.

3. In a small skillet over low heat, add the olive oil and saute the red onion about 3 minutes. Add to the peppers.

4. Drain the raisins, discarding any leftover tequila, and add to the relish with the remaining ingredients. Mix well and reserve at room temperature until ready to serve.

GRAPEFRUIT-ORANGE SALSA

This colorful combination of citrus fruits makes a perfect condiment for fish tacos. The serranos add just the right chile kick. If serving a main dish intense with chile flavors, reduce the serranos so the salsa cools the palate.

Yield: 6 servings

3 large oranges, peeled and sectioned

2 large Ruby Red grapefruits, peeled and sectioned

1/3 cup coarsely chopped fresh cilantro

1 to 2 serrano chiles, minced (optional)

1 red onion, trimmed and cut into slivers

Extra virgin olive oil to taste

Balsamic or red wine vinegar to taste

Salt to taste

1. Combine all ingredients except the oil, vinegar, and salt; mix gently. Add the remaining ingredients no more than 5 minutes before serving (the acid will make the citrus sections fall apart).

Serving suggestion: This salsa is a perfect side dish for duck and Monterey jack quesadillas.

ROASTED TOMATO SALSA

The flavor of this salsa is best in the summer, using red ripe tomatoes just picked from the vine. The tomatoes can easily be roasted on your outdoor grill in place of a stove-top grill. This salsa tastes terrific with just about anything; but for a real treat, try it with grilled lamb and fresh corn, or spoon over scrambled eggs for a whole new breakfast experience.

Yield: about 3 cups

2 pounds ripe plum tomatoes

3 garlic cloves, minced

1 large red onion, finely diced

2 to 3 serrano chiles, minced, or
    2 tablespoons pureed chipotle
    chiles in adobo sauce to taste

1/3 cup coarsely chopped fresh
    cilantro

1 teaspoon dried Mexican oregano,
    crushed

Splash of balsamic vinegar to taste

Coarse salt to taste

Pinch of sugar (optional)

Extra virgin olive oil to taste

1. Place a stove-top grill over high flame and char the plum tomatoes on all sides. Put them in a medium bowl and set aside to cool.

2. Peel and core the tomatoes. Place the tomatoes and their juices in the work bowl of a food processor and pulse to a coarse puree, keeping the tomatoes as chunky as possible. Pour the puree into a medium bowl. Add the garlic, onion, chile, cilantro, and oregano; season to taste with vinegar, salt, and sugar. Let stand for 20 minutes. Taste and adjust seasoning. Drizzle with a little olive oil, stir, and serve.

SALSA FRESCA

Before the opening of the Santa Fe School of Cooking in December 1989, Bill Weiland, current director of the culinary arts program at the Santa Fe Community College, was hired to help develop the first few recipes for the school. Susan Curtis, her husband David, and Bill congregated to test and taste a number of recipes. This "basic" fresh tomato salsa is one of the first recipes used at the school and is still very popular. Bill still makes this salsa and serves it with chips or on tacos, enchiladas, or fajitas.

Yield: about 2-1/2 cups

4 to 5 plum tomatoes, diced

1/2 cup finely chopped red onion

1 teaspoon dried Mexican oregano, crushed

2 serrano chiles, finely chopped

1 teaspoon minced garlic (optional)

3 tablespoons coarsely chopped fresh cilantro

2 to 3 tablespoons fresh lime juice or cider vinegar

1 tablespoon olive oil (optional)

Salt to taste

Pinch of sugar (optional)

1. Put the tomatoes, onion, oregano, chiles, garlic, and cilantro in a bowl and mix well.

2. Add the lime juice or cider vinegar, olive oil, salt, and sugar to taste. Let the mixture sit for 20 minutes to meld the flavors.

SALSA ROUGE

Allen Smith was introduced to Salsa Rouge while a culinary student in France. As a guest at an Italian friend's house, he was served fettucini with olive oil and ground veal. At each place was a small ramekin of *salsa rouge*, similar to this delicious mixture. It makes a flavorful garnish for any meat or poultry, or can be used successfully as a quick sauce to spoon over pasta.

Yield: 2 cups

1 red bell pepper, roasted, peeled, seeded, and diced

1 cup diced ripe tomato

1/2 cup chopped, oil-packed sundried tomatoes

1/3 cup chopped fresh basil

2 to 3 tablespoons red wine vinegar

2 to 3 tablespoons extra virgin olive oil

Salt to taste

Pinch of sugar to taste

1. Combine all ingredients and let stand for 30 minutes. Taste and correct seasonings. Serve.

OLIVE-TOMATO SALSA

Santa Fe Cooking School instructor and cookbook author Janet Mitchell created this interesting garnish for grilled meats and fish. It could also be a quick tasty topping to spoon over pasta.

Yield: about 2 cups

4 ripe plum tomatoes, diced

1/3 cup pitted, sliced Kalamata olives

2 scallions, thinly sliced

1 garlic clove, minced

2 tablespoons chopped fresh basil

1/2 teaspoon dried Mexican oregano

4 tablespoons extra virgin olive oil

2 tablespoons balsamic or red wine vinegar

Coarse salt and freshly ground black pepper to taste

1. Mix together the tomatoes, olives, scallions, garlic, basil, and oregano in a serving bowl.

2. Whisk together the oil, vinegar, salt, and pepper, and drizzle over the salsa. Stir thoroughly and let stand for 20 minutes. Taste and adjust seasoning. Serve.

⊚ INGREDIENTS ⊚

Avocado — Oval-shaped fruit with a greenish, buttery-tasting flesh. The Hass avocado, with its bumpy brownish-black skin, is the preferred variety for taste. To ripen, leave at room temperature for a day or two, or place in a paper bag to hasten.

Chicos — Corn that has been partially shucked, roasted on the cob, dried, and removed from the cob. The result is a chewy but flavorful kernel requiring a long cooking time.

Cilantro — Fresh plant from the coriander seed; however, it is not interchangeable with the seed. It is a delicate, aromatic herb of the parsley family. To store, recut the stem ends and place in shallow water. Cover with a plastic bag and store in the refrigerator. Readily available in most grocery stores.

Epazote — A pungent herb that grows wild in Mexico and the United States. It is used frequently in seasoning beans and also acts as an anti-flatulent for beans.

Huitlacoche, or **cuitlacoche** — A silvery-grey to black fungus, commonly known as smut in the United States, that is cultivated in the kernels of corn. The puffy kernels, or lobes, can be detached from the ears and kept refrigerated for several days. It is usually found frozen or canned and is considered a delicacy in Mexico.

Jicama — A tan-skinned tuber. The flavor of the crisp white flesh is compared to that of a water chestnut or a sweet radish. Primarily used uncooked.

Mexican Oregano — A weedy-flavored herb reminiscent of, but distinctly different from, the more common Mediterranean oregano. It is used in the dry whole-leaf form vs. the ground form.

Mexican Vanilla Bean — The pod of a tropical orchid vine. It is native to the New World, dating back to the Aztec culture.

New Mexican or **Southwestern Piñon Nuts** — Similar to imported pine nuts but much richer in flavor and oil. They should be stored in the freezer to preserve freshness.

Nopales — Cactus paddles or the paddle-shaped stems from several varieties of the prickly pear cactus plants. The flavor is somewhat similar to a green bean. They are commonly used in Mexican and southwestern cooking.

Posole — Dried corn that has been boiled in a hydrate-lime solution to remove the husk, resulting in an increase in the nutrient value. Used extensively in the Southwest as a side dish or soup.

Tomatillo — A tart green fruit used frequently in Mexican sauces. In appearance only, it resembles a small green tomato in papery husks. It is a close relative of the cape gooseberry that grows wild in the United States. Fresh tomatillos are available in most grocery stores.

⚙ COOKING TERMINOLOGY AND EQUIPMENT ⚙

Chiffonade — The cutting of leafy greens or herbs into thin, even strips.

Stove-Top Grill — The Santa Fe School of Cooking manufactures a grill that sits on top of electric and gas ranges. It can be used to roast chiles, bell peppers, tomatoes, and more in place of using the outdoor grill or oven. Many of the recipes in this book call for roasting chiles, peppers, garlic, etc., and may mention the use of this grill. It has become an essential tool for cooking at the school.

⚙ CHILES ⚙

Ancho — Wrinkled, heart-shaped, dark cranberry red chile that is the dried form of the fresh poblano. Mild to medium heat level with sweet dried-fruit flavors reminiscent of prunes, figs, and tobacco.

Chipotle — Dried and smoked form of a fresh jalapeño chile; dusty brown in color.

Chipotle Chiles in Adobo Sauce — Chipotle chiles in a sauce consisting primarily of tomatoes, vinegar, garlic, onion, and spices.

Habanero — Extremely hot but flavorful lantern-shaped chile with fruity, flowery aroma; used extensively in the Yucatan. Freezes easily without changing flavor or texture.

Morita — Dried smoked jalapeño, reddish in color.

New Mexico Red Chiles — A form of the green chile that has ripened to its red state and dried. It may be used as pods, crushed (caribe), or as a finely ground powder.

Poblano — An all-purpose dark green fresh chile with a heat varying from mild to hot. Very full flavored and commonly used for rajas and chile rellenos.

Serrano — Fresh, small green chile, cylindrical in shape and measuring approximately 1 to 2 inches long and 1/2 to 3/4 inch wide. It is a crisp hot chile used extensively in salsas.

RESOURCES

Chile Today Hot Tamale
(mail order only)
2-D Great Meadow Lane
East Hanover, NJ 07936
(800) 468-7377
Web site: www.chiletoday.com
— *Dried chiles, hot sauces, and chile powders.*

Dean & Deluca
1. Catalog Department
(800) 221-7714
Web site: www.deandeluca.com
— *Dried chiles, dried posole, spices, hot sauces.*

2. 560 Broadway
New York, NY 10012
(212) 226-6800

3. 3276 M Street NW
Washington, DC 20007
(202) 342-2500

El Paso Chile Company
909 Texas Avenue
El Paso, TX 79901
(800) 274-7468
Web site: www.elpasochile.com
— *Bottled sauces, dips, pestos, etc.*

Kalustyan's
123 Lexington Avenue
   (between 28th & 29th)
New York, NY 10016
(212) 685-3451
Web site: www.kalustyans.com
— *Asian, Indian, and Mexican spices; nuts, dried fruit, grains, beans, and chile powders.*

Mo Hotta Mo Betta
(mail order only)
P.O. Box 4136
San Luis Obispo, CA 93406
(800) 462-3220
Web site: www.mohotta.com
— *Dried chiles, herbs, spices, hot sauces, and salsa.*

Pendery's, Inc.
1221 Manufacturing Street
Dallas, TX 75207
(800) 533-1870
(214) 741-1870
Web site: www.penderys.com
— *Dried chiles and spices.*

Santa Fe School of Cooking
116 West San Francisco Street
Santa Fe, NM 87501
(800) 982-4688
(505) 983-4511
(505) 983-7540 fax
Web site:
www.santafeschoolofcooking.com
— *Over twenty varieties of dried chiles and powders, huitlacoche, chipotle chiles in adobo, herbs, spices, posole, Mexican chocolate, and more.*

⊙ ACKNOWLEDGMENTS ⊙

We would like to express our appreciation to past and present chefs of the Santa Fe School of Cooking for contributing their recipes and ideas. They include Janet Mitchell, Allen Smith, David Jones, Bill Weiland, James Campbell, Zach Calkins, and Peter Zimmer. We are most indebted to the staff at the school for all of their support, including tasting, input, and proofreading. A very special thanks to photographer Lois Ellen Frank and to her wonderful assistant, Walter Whitewater, for not only producing such great photographs but for making the food photography such a fun experience. There are too many taste testers to list all, but special acknowledgments to Cheryl Alters Jamison, Lois Stouffer, and Ellen Stelling. Marcia Jarrett provided kitchen assistance beyond the call of friendship.

Props for the photography were provided by Lois Ellen Frank and the Santa Fe School of Cooking, as well as Cookworks of Santa Fe, New Mexico; Bal Harbour, Florida; and Dallas, Texas. Contact Cookworks at (800) 972-3357.

∅ INDEX ∅

Ancho chiles, 40

Avocado: and tomatillo salsa, 16–17; defined, 39

Bean salsa, 8–9

Caribe, 40

Cherry and pistachio salsa, 22–23

Chicos: posole and onion salsa, 25–26; defined, 39

Chiffonade, 40

Chile heat—hot (muy picante) or 3-chile dishes, 11, 27

Chile heat—medium (picante) or 2-chile dishes, 6, 7, 8–9, 10, 12–13, 14–15, 16–17, 19, 22–23, 28–29, 32–33, 34, 35

Chile heat—mild (suave) or 1-chile dishes, 1–3, 4–5, 18, 20–21, 24, 25–26, 30, 31, 36–37, 38

Chipotle chiles, 14, 40

Chipotle chiles in adobo sauce, 40

Cilantro, 39

Corn, roasted: and huitlacoche relish, 6; and bean salsa, 8–9

Cucumber salsa, 28–29

Cuitlacoche, 39

Epazote, 39

Fruit relishes/salsas, 4–5, 10, 12–13, 19, 20–21, 22–23, 24, 31, 32–33

Grapefruit and orange salsa, 32–33

Habanero chiles, 11; and kumquat relish, 12–13; and onions, 27; defined, 40

Huitlacoche: and corn salsa, 6; defined, 39

Jicama: and watermelon salsa, 24; defined, 39

Kumquat and habanero relish, 12–13

Mango salsa, 19

Morita chiles, 40

New Mexico red chiles: salsa, 14–15; defined, 40

Nopal/Nopales: and poblano salsa, 1–3; defined, 39

Olive and tomato salsa, 38

Onions: pickled red, 18; chicos and posole salsa, 25–26; habanero pickled, 27

Orange and grapefruit salsa, 32–33

Oregano, Mexican, 39

Papaya and tomatillo salsa, 10

Pepper, bell: rajas salsa, 30; raisins and piñon nut relish, 31

Pineapple salsa, 20–21

Piñon nuts, New Mexican/southwestern: peppers and raisins salsa, 31; defined, 39

Pistachio and bing cherry salsa, 22–23

Poblano chiles: and nopal salsa, 1; defined, 40

Posole: chicos and onions salsa, 25–26; defined, 39

Rajas, 30

Relishes, 6, 24, 31

Raisins, peppers, and piñon nut relish, 31

Salsa: definition of, iv; Fresca, 35; Rouge, 36–37

Serrano chiles, 40

Stove-Top Grill, 40

Tomatillo: salsa, 7; and papaya salsa, 10; and avocado salsa, 16–17; defined, 39

Tomato: salsa, 34; and olive salsa, 38

Vanilla bean, Mexican, 39

Watermelon and jicama salsa, 24

⑨ SANTA FE SCHOOL OF COOKING AND MARKET ⑨

The Santa Fe School of Cooking is a regional cooking school that opened its doors in December 1989. Since its opening, thousands of guests have enjoyed taking classes, participating in culinary tours, and becoming part of the school's family. The adjacent market specializes in local products and has its own product line. A mail-order catalog is also available.

If you would like to receive information about the Santa Fe School of Cooking, please copy and fill out this form, then mail to the following address:

The Santa Fe School of Cooking
116 West San Francisco Street
Santa Fe, NM 87501
(800) 982-4688 catalog information
(505) 983-4511 class information
(505) 983-7540 fax

Check out our Web site for a current class schedule, information about culinary tours, special events, or shopping on-line: *www.santafeschoolofcooking.com*

Name _____

Address _____

City _____ State _____ Zip Code _____

Phone _____